Drought and Heat Wave Alert!

Paul Challen

Crabtree Publishing Company
www.crabtreebooks.com

DISASTER ALERT!

presented by:

Crabtree Publishing Company
www.crabtreebooks.com

For Sam, Evelina, and Henry

Coordinating editor: Ellen Rodger

Project editor: Rachel Eagen

Book design and production coordinator: Rosie Gowsell

Cover design: Rob MacGregor

Photo research: Allison Napier

Consultants: Mark Svoboda, National Drought Mitigation Center, University of Nebraska-Lincoln; Douglas Le Comte, National Oceanic and Atmospheric Administration (NOAA)

Photographs: AFP/ Getty Image: p. 22 (top); AP/ Wide World Photos: p. 6 (bottom left), p. 7 (bottom), p. 9 (top), p. 13, p. 14 (top right), p. 15 (top), p. 16 (both), p. 17 (bottom), p. 21, p. 24, p. 25 (top), p. 26 (bottom), p. 27 (top), p. 28, p. 29 (both); Dan Carnemolla/Australian Picture Library/ CORBIS: p. 4; Charles O. Cecil: p. 6 (top right); Nigel Dennis/ Photo researchers, Inc: p. 3; Martin Dohrn/ Photo Researchers, Inc: p. 15 (left); Mike England/ Photo Researchers, Inc: p. 27 (bottom); David R. Frazer/ Photo Researchers, Inc: p. 9 (bottom); Mark Henley/ Panos Pictures: p. 17 (top right); Thomas Jouanneau/ CORBIS SYGMA: p. 19; Mian Khursheed/ Reuters: p. 12; Rick Maiman/ CORBIS SYGMA: p. 8; National Oceanic and Atmospheric Administration: p. 14 (left); Chip Simmons/ Getty Images: p. 1; Peter Skinner/ Photo Researchers, Inc: p. 20; Les Stone/ CORBIS: p. 5 (top), p. 26 (top); Ami Vitale/ Panos Pictures: p. 18

Illustrations: Dan Pressman: p. 7 (top), pp. 10-11, p. 23; David Wysotski, Allure Illustrations: pp. 30-31

Cover: Streams and rivers dry up during a drought, so animals have to move in search of fresh water to drink. If animals do not find a fresh water source, they will die from dehydration.

Title page: Concrete gets so hot during a heat wave that it can fry an egg.

Contents: Droughts cause the soil to become parched and cracked.

Crabtree Publishing Company
www.crabtreebooks.com   1-800-387-7650

Copyright © 2005 CRABTREE PUBLISHING COMPANY. All rights reserved. No part of this publication may be reproduced, stored in a retrieval system or transmitted in any form or by any means, electronic, mechanical, photocopying, recording, or otherwise, without the prior written permission of Crabtree Publishing Company. In Canada: We acknowledge the financial support of the Government of Canada through the Book Publishing Industry Development Program (BPIDP) for our publishing activities.

Cataloging-in-Publication data

Challen, Paul C. (Paul Clarence), 1967-
  Drought and heat wave alert! / written by Paul Challen.
    p. cm. -- (Disaster alert!)
    Includes index.
  ISBN 0-7787-1578-7 (rlb) -- ISBN 0-7787-1610-4 (pbk)
  1. Droughts--Juvenile literature. 2. Heat waves (Meteorology)-- Juvenile literature. I. Title. II. Series.
  QC929.25.C47 2005
  551.57'73--dc22
                                        2004013054
                                        LC

**Published in
the United States**
PMB 16A
350 Fifth Ave.
Suite 3308
New York, NY
10118

**Published
in Canada**
616 Welland Ave.,
St. Catharines,
Ontario, Canada
L2M 5V6

**Published in the
United Kingdom**
73 Lime Walk
Headington
Oxford
0X3 7AD
United Kingdom

**Published
in Australia**
386 Mt. Alexander Rd.,
Ascot Vale (Melbourne)
V1C 3032

Table of Contents

Dry as Dust

Water is the basis of all life on Earth. Without water, people, animals, and plants cannot survive. Drought is a period of time when there is less rain, snow, or other forms of precipitation, than normal. Droughts are often accompanied by prolonged heat, or heat waves.

Without water

Droughts develop over long periods of time. Some droughts last several years and some are seasonal. Scientists who study the moisture in the Earth generally agree that a drought is a period of time when precipitation levels are so low that they reduce the water supply and affect agriculture. The extreme heat of a heat wave often dries out sources of water, including streams and rivers.

What is a disaster?
A disaster is a destructive event that affects the natural world and human communities. Some disasters are predictable and others occur without warning. Coping successfully with a disaster depends on a community's preparation.

Droughts cause water-starved animals and plants to die from dehydration. In 2002, a drought in Australia killed many animals, including this kangaroo.

Farmers use water to nourish their crops and livestock, while people use it for drinking, bathing, recreation, and travel. Rain helps this farmer's crops to grow.

Drought Gods

In many ancient cultures, people thought that certain gods, goddesses, and other mythical beings were responsible for creating droughts. In Australia, aboriginal people tell a legend about a giant frog who once sucked up all of the water and held it in his mouth, causing a terrible drought. When the other animals made the frog laugh, the water poured from his mouth and over the land in a great flood. The water made the land green and created plentiful lakes and rivers for the people. Some drought myths continue today, and people try and protect their land. Traditionally, in parts of India, villagers sacrificed animals to the gods who were believed to cause dry spells. Sacrifices were thought to protect the people, as they pleased the gods and prevented them from causing droughts and suffering.

Barren Lands

A drought begins with a disruption to the water cycle, the circulation of water from the Earth's atmosphere to its surface. Sometimes this disruption happens naturally, such as during a heat wave. Most droughts are temporary, and can occur in all climates. Some climates are permanently dry, or arid, such as deserts.

How droughts happen

A drought is a shortage of precipitation over a period of time. Droughts get worse when rivers and streams dry up, leaving people without water to drink and to grow food. Droughts should not be confused with arid climates, where very little precipitation falls year round. A drought happens when a specific geographic region receives much less precipitation than normal. Conditions that are thought to be drought-like in North America might not be considered drought-like in Africa or parts of Australia. In arid climates, people have developed ways of surviving with very little water. They also **conserve** what little water they have.

(above) In arid countries, farmers build channels to collect water from mountain streams or other sources, to irrigate their crops.

(left) A farmer waters his crops in Cambodia. Watering after sunset helps to reduce water waste. Heat from the sun causes water to evaporate, or turn from a liquid to a gas.

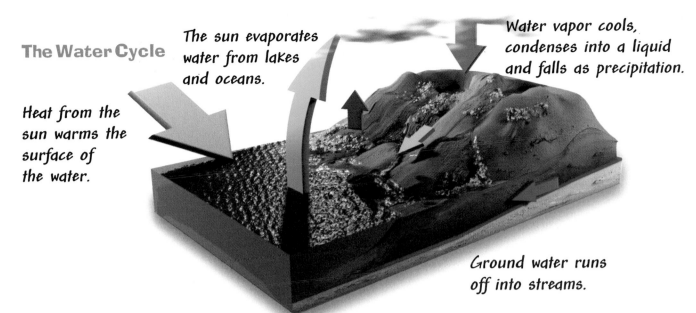

The Water Cycle

The sun evaporates water from lakes and oceans.

Water vapor cools, condenses into a liquid and falls as precipitation.

Heat from the sun warms the surface of the water.

Ground water runs off into streams.

Droughts and the water cycle

The water cycle sustains all life on Earth, because it is the system through which humans, animals, and plants receive the water they need to survive and grow. The water cycle begins when the sun heats water on the Earth's surface, from oceans, lakes, rivers, and streams. The heat causes the **molecules** that make up water to move more quickly and rise into the air as a gas, a process called **evaporation**. As water vapor rises, it cools off and **condenses** to form clouds. When the clouds have become too heavy to hold any more water, precipitation falls in the form of rain, snow, or hail. As the precipitation falls back to Earth, some of it returns to rivers and other water sources. Some water soaks into the ground, through the soil, and into layers of rock under the ground, called aquifers. Droughts happen when the water cycle is disrupted. The disruption can happen in several different ways, including when the weather is so hot that the water evaporates too quickly to fall as rain.

Droughts can ruin entire crops of food, leaving people to go hungry. This Guatemalan farmer holds damaged corn from his field. A drought affecting parts of South America in 2001 caused 1.4 million people to suffer from *malnutrition*, because the shortage of rain prevented food crops from growing.

Getting Warmer

A heat wave begins when the temperature reaches uncomfortably high levels, generally 90° Fahrenheit (32° Celsius) or more. Heat waves can last anywhere from two to five days or several weeks, and they usually occur during the warm summer months. Heat waves are often accompanied by drought or abnormally dry weather.

Temperature and air pressure

Heat waves usually occur when the winds and breezes that normally move air around and cool it, are not present. As the temperature rises, the molecules that make up air move more quickly, and rise into the atmosphere. As air molecules cool, they slow down and sink back toward the Earth.

Air pressure, or atmospheric pressure, is the force of air that presses against other objects on Earth. Air moves in masses from areas of **high pressure** to areas of **low pressure**. Wind currents are created by the movement of air as it heats and cools, moving from high pressure areas to lower pressure areas.

Swimming or resting in a shady place helps people feel more comfortable when the temperature soars. Cooling off at the beach is one way to beat the heat.

Heat waves and humidity

Humidity is the amount of moisture, or water vapor, in the air. In weather reports, humidity is expressed as a percentage and is called "relative humidity." This percentage refers to how much water the air can hold at the current temperature.

Heat and humidity build up under a dome of high air pressure. High air pressure blocks cooler air from rushing into a region, and also causes the air to grow still. Temperatures and humidity rise when there are few wind currents to move the heat around.

Fans circulate the air and help people feel cooler.

The Greenhouse Effect

The Greenhouse Effect describes what happens when the sun's heat is trapped by the gases in the Earth's atmosphere. Normally, gases in the atmosphere allow sunshine to pass through but absorb the heat back from the surface of the Earth. The trapped gases increase the Earth's temperature. This is known as global warming. Global warming worries scientists because they think that when the Earth becomes too warm, the planet's climate will change, leading to more droughts and floods.

Smog traps hot air close to the ground, increasing the effects of greenhouse gases.

Name That Drought

All droughts are called meteorological droughts. Meteorological drought occurs when less precipitation falls than is normal for a region at a specific time of year. Scientists label droughts according to how they affect people and the water supply. Since drought affects people in many different ways, droughts may fall into more than one category at the same time.

Hydrological drought

A hydrological drought is a physical drought where scientists compare the amount of moisture in the soil to the amount of precipitation that normally falls. They also measure the amount of water in surface and subsurface water supplies such as streams, reservoirs, or aquifers.

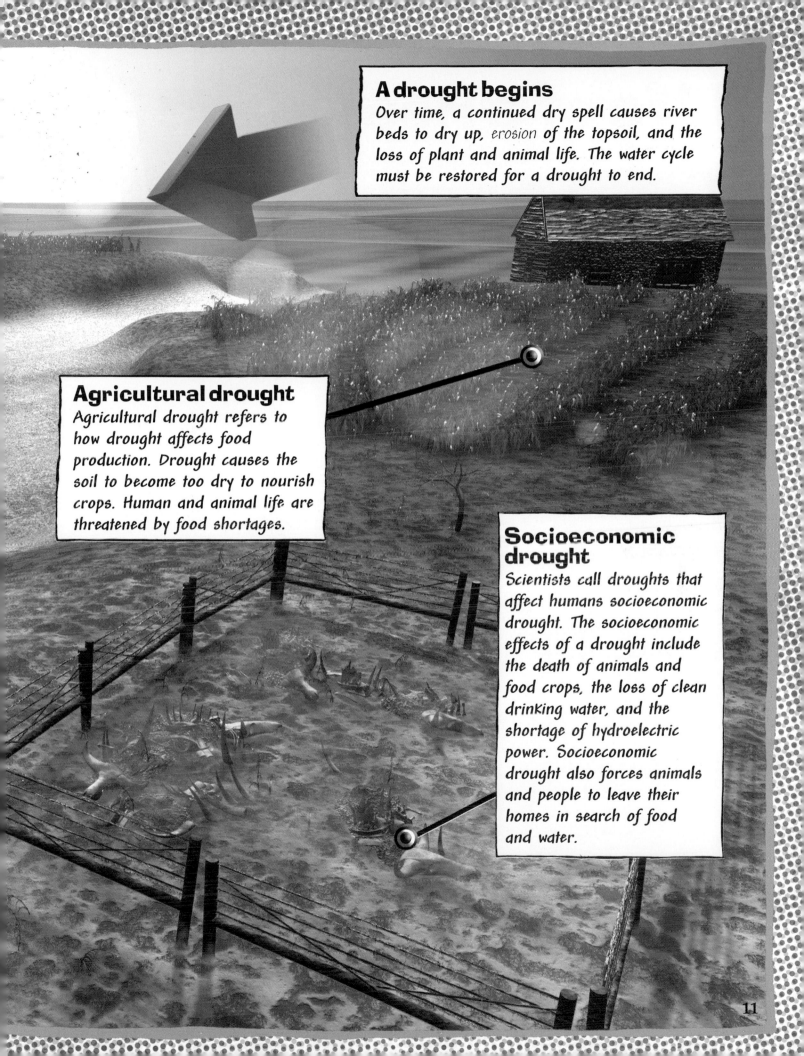

A drought begins
Over time, a continued dry spell causes river beds to dry up, *erosion* of the topsoil, and the loss of plant and animal life. The water cycle must be restored for a drought to end.

Agricultural drought
Agricultural drought refers to how drought affects food production. Drought causes the soil to become too dry to nourish crops. Human and animal life are threatened by food shortages.

Socioeconomic drought
Scientists call droughts that affect humans socioeconomic drought. The socioeconomic effects of a drought include the death of animals and food crops, the loss of clean drinking water, and the shortage of hydroelectric power. Socioeconomic drought also forces animals and people to leave their homes in search of food and water.

11

Life of a Heat Wave

Heat waves are long periods of extremely hot temperatures that are often accompanied by high humidity. Heat waves occur in many of the world's climates.

Rise in temperature

Weather scientists, or meteorologists, define a heat wave as a rise in temperature that lasts over a period of time. Uncomfortably high temperatures during a heat wave can kill people. The elderly and the sick are most likely to die during a heat wave. Heat waves can last for a few days or several weeks.

How weather gets so hot

Long periods of high temperatures create heat waves. Heat waves happen because of atmospheric pressure. Atmospheric pressure is the weight of the Earth's atmosphere. A rise in atmospheric pressure creates the high temperatures of a heat wave. High pressure **compresses** the air, causing it to heat up. High air pressure also prevents rain clouds from forming. Stagnant, or unmoving, air thickens the atmosphere, trapping pollutants in busy cities.

Heat waves are especially brutal in hot countries such as Pakistan. These men cool off on blocks of ice during a heat wave.

Dry as bone...

Heat sucks moisture out of soil, making the dirt much lighter. Lighter soil can be picked up by the wind and blown around in clouds of swirling dust and sand called dust storms. The lack of moisture in soil causes plants to wilt and die.

People also suffer during heat waves because heat causes them to sweat, bringing water to their skin instead of keeping it inside the body. In both plants and animals, severe lack of moisture is called dehydration.

The end of a heat wave

A cool mass of air blowing in from a large body of water usually ends a heat wave. Storm clouds full of cool, condensed water bring much-needed relief from hot temperatures. In 1999, the northeastern United States suffered a heat wave that caused temperatures to soar above 100° Fahrenheit (38° Celsius). The use of air conditioners and electric fans created an extra demand for power, causing blackouts. Cool weather blew in from the Atlantic to end the heat wave, but severe storms with high winds resulted when the cold and hot air mixed.

Urban heat island effect

Asphalt and concrete can store heat for long periods. These substances absorb heat during the day, then release it back into the atmosphere once the sun sets. The added heat at night creates the urban heat island effect, in which cities experience higher night time temperatures than rural areas. The effects of a heat wave are often felt more severely in cities, as there is no heat break from sunrise to sunset.

High temperatures heat the asphalt and cement that hold structures together, causing them to weaken and crack.

Mercury Rising...

Throughout history, there have been many catastrophic droughts and heat waves that have devastated entire regions, causing mass migrations of people to different areas, and thousands of deaths.

High winds and parched soil created enormous dust storms during the Dust Bowl. Homes and farmland were destroyed over the decade-long drought, causing many people to move westward in search of more hospitable land.

The Dust Bowl

The plains and prairies of the United States and Canada suffered a serious drought during an eight-year stretch in the 1930s. The areas from Texas to Kansas, and from Manitoba to Alberta, were good agricultural land. A period of low rainfall combined with **overfarming** caused this large area to become very dry and dusty, as the top layer of soil dried up and blew around in the high winds of the plains. People suffered as large clouds of dust swirled around for days, making breathing very difficult and setting foot outdoors dangerous. By the mid-1930s, millions of acres of land had become unsuitable for growing food. Farmers and their families were forced to abandon their land. The drought came to an end in 1939, when rain saturated the land and made it useful once again.

Drought in the Sahel

In the mid-1980s, drought struck the Sahel, a region between the Sahara desert and the tropical rainforests in central North Africa. In most years, the Sahel is dry between October and June, but people who live there have developed a water-delivery system to last them through this dry season. The delivery system is a network of canals and **irrigation** channels that were built to ensure the flow of water through populated areas. During the mid-1980s, a series of wars broke out in Ethiopia, Somalia, and the Sudan that disrupted this system. Millions of people were forced to leave their homes to trek across the Sahel in search of water. It is estimated that almost one million people died from starvation and disease between 1984 and 1985. Millions of farm animals also died during this time, causing herders to lose their source of income.

Droughts in the Sahel region of Africa over the last two decades have caused the suffering of animals, humans, and vegetation. These cattle are starving because there is not enough water to nourish the crops to feed them.

15

Heat waves in India

India experienced a terrible heat wave in the spring of 2002. Temperatures reached higher than 110° Fahrenheit (44° Celsius) between May and June. Widespread power shortages were caused by the overuse of fans and air conditioners. Blackouts left people unable to cool off, and hospitals were filled with people suffering a number of heat illnesses such as heat cramps and heat stroke. Almost 1,200 people died from the extreme weather.

Strenuous activities should be avoided during a heat wave. These people rest together on the cool floor of a train station in southern India.

Dehydration, overexposure from the sun, or a lack of cooling mechanisms such as air conditioning or pools can all cause heat illness or even death in severe heat. This father and son visit the graves of several victims after a heat wave struck Chicago in 1995.

Drought in China

A terrible period of drought led to the deaths of nine to thirteen million people in northern China between 1876 and 1879. Rice farmers in the region depend on heavy rains and flooding that are brought by the summer **monsoon**. During this period, the wet monsoon brought much less rain than usual. About 600,000 square miles (one million square km) were without an adequate water supply. Crops failed and people starved. A few decades later, in the 1920s, a drought brought on by similar circumstances hit the same part of China, causing approximately 500,000 deaths.

The Yellow River, one of China's oldest and most important sources of water, dries up during a drought. The river is responsible for irrigating crops that feed millions of people.

During a drought, the land becomes so dry that the soil is picked up and carried great distances. The dusty air hurts the skin, lowers visibility, and causes breathing problems.

Forecasting

Centuries ago, ancient Egyptians believed that the planet Mars controlled flooding of the Nile River. Today, scientists consider many factors when forecasting droughts and heat waves. Factors include: the amount of precipitation that is expected to fall, how hot the temperatures will be, and how long these conditions will last.

Monitoring drought

Scientists monitor weather conditions and analyze soil moisture and water use. One of the most common tools used to assess drought is called the Palmer Drought Index, which measures what is known as "supply and demand soil moisture." Supply refers to how much moisture is in the soil. Demand refers to how much moisture the soil needs to support plant growth. In areas where the supply of soil moisture is low and the demand for soil moisture is high, the Palmer Drought Index will show that drought is likely.

Predicting heat waves

Meteorologists collect and analyze records of heat, humidity, and heat-related deaths to determine high risk regions for heat waves. Before a heat wave, **advisories** are placed in newspapers and on television. People are warned to stay indoors and to drink fluids. Community workers and volunteers set up information hotlines and air-conditioned shelters.

The desert supports vegetation that has adapted to thrive in dry soil.

Women in the Tigre region of Ethiopia dig in the parched river bed, searching for water beneath the ground. Frequent droughts have threatened the farming and herding lifestyle of the people in the area. Resettlement programs began in 2002, to relocate people to more hospitable land.

Drought devastation

The effects of drought are economic, environmental, and social. The most dangerous effect of droughts is that people cannot get enough to eat and drink. Damage to crops means food will be scarce. What little food there is will be expensive. People who cannot afford to pay must beg for food and water, or rely on assistance from international aid agencies. The extreme heat that often accompanies drought can lead to fires. Hot, dry conditions also cause **infestations** of insects, which may carry diseases.

In drought-prone regions, conflicts may break out over who owns water supplies, and how relief should be distributed. Sometimes, there is simply not enough resources to reach all of those in need. When this happens, people move long distances in search of more water. This can be dangerous for people who are already weak from going without food and water for a long time.

The Drought Monitor

In the United States, the National Drought Mitigation Center, the United States Department of Agriculture (USDA), and the National Oceanic and Atmospheric Administration (NOAA) developed the Drought Monitor to monitor droughts. The Drought Monitor is a series of maps that chart climatic regions and their vulnerability to drought. Color-coded areas on the maps indicate the potential risk and severity of drought, based on crop damage, water levels, seasonal temperatures, soil moisture, and water restrictions that are in place.

Keeping Your Cool

High temperatures and high humidity can feel very uncomfortable. Heat illnesses, such as heat cramps, heat exhaustion, and heat stroke, result after spending a long time in the heat or sun. People who live in high-risk areas for heat waves need to know how to treat heat illnesses.

Heat cramps

Heat cramps occur when muscles contract, or tense up. Heat cramps result when the body has lost too much water and salt through sweating. Muscles need both salt and water to function properly. Heat cramps often occur in the large muscles at the back of the leg, and can be very painful. They can be eased by drinking water, stretching the affected muscles, and resting in a shady area or in an air-conditioned building.

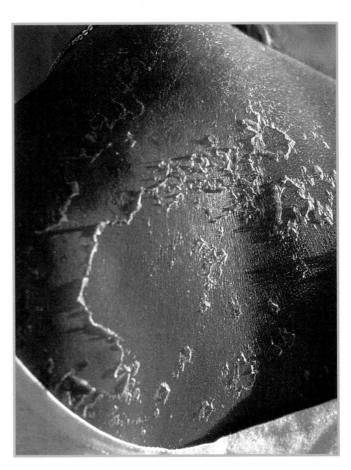

Skin that is unprotected by clothing or sun block is more likely to get burned by the sun's powerful rays. Peeling, flaking, and blistering are common reactions to overexposure to the sun.

Heat Index

High temperatures feel even hotter when the air is humid. Meteorologists developed a chart known as the Heat Index (H.I.), which explains how hot the weather actually feels, taking into account both temperature and humidity. For example, a day that is 90° Fahrenheit (32° Celsius), with a relative humidity level of 78 percent, feels like 117° Fahrenheit (47° Celsius) to the human body. Heat advisories are issued when the Heat Index values are forecast to reach 105° Fahrenheit (41° Celsius), since these are dangerous temperatures.

Heat exhaustion

Heat exhaustion happens after people are exposed to high temperatures, without drinking enough fluids. People suffering from heat exhaustion have increased heart rates and heavy sweating. Other symptoms of heat exhaustion are paleness, muscle cramps, dizziness, headaches, nausea, vomiting, or fainting. It is important to cool off a person suffering from heat exhaustion by moving them to a cool place, placing them in a cool bath, and providing fluids to drink.

Dehydration due to heat stroke is so severe that patients are fed a solution of vital nutrients through a needle, called an intravenous tube.

Heat stroke

Heat stroke is the most serious of all the heat illnesses. A person suffering from heat stroke has already lost the fluids needed to produce sweat to cool off. If a person's body temperature continues to rise 7° Fahrenheit (14° Celsius) or higher within ten to fifteen minutes, they are suffering from heat stroke. People suffering from heat stroke develop red, hot and dry skin. Their heartbeat increases, and they suffer from severe headaches, nausea, dizziness, or unconsciousness. Treatment includes applying cool water to the body while fanning the skin to imitate sweating. Ice packs should be applied to the groin and armpits to cool the person down. People with heat stroke should be treated by a doctor at a hospital or clinic.

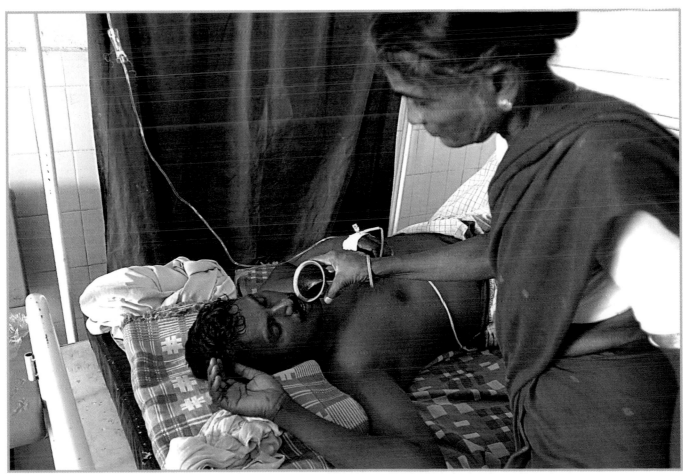

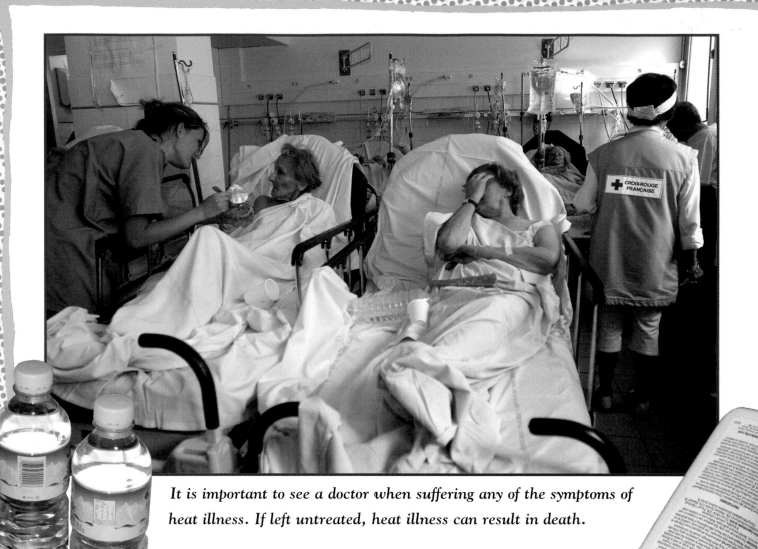

It is important to see a doctor when suffering any of the symptoms of heat illness. If left untreated, heat illness can result in death.

Staying safe in hot weather

There are several ways that people can keep cool in hot weather. During hot weather people should remain indoors or in a cool place whenever possible, and try to avoid direct sunlight. If you have to go outside, wear loose, lightweight, and light-colored clothing as well as a hat to block the sun's rays. Be sure to wear lots of sun block. Keep hydrated by drinking water, even if you are not thirsty. Avoid soda, or soft drinks, and heavy foods, as these put the body at greater risk of dehydration. Strenuous activities should be avoided, since they raise the body's temperature and increase sweating, or water loss. Take a cool swim or shower to lower your body temperature. It is important to tell an adult if the heat is making you feel ill. Most local radio and television stations broadcast information about heat risks and what to do to stay safe. News bulletins inform people when it is too hot to go outside and advise people on how to conserve water and power.

Heat and the human body

1. High temperatures, humidity, and exposure to the sun warm the body. Physical activity also increases the body's temperature.

2. The brain sends signals to different parts of the body to help it cool down.

3. The body's core gets very warm. This includes the groin and armpits.

4. Heat spreads out, traveling to the body's extremities (arms, legs, and feet).

5. The body sweats to cool down.

6. Panting further helps the body to get rid of extra heat.

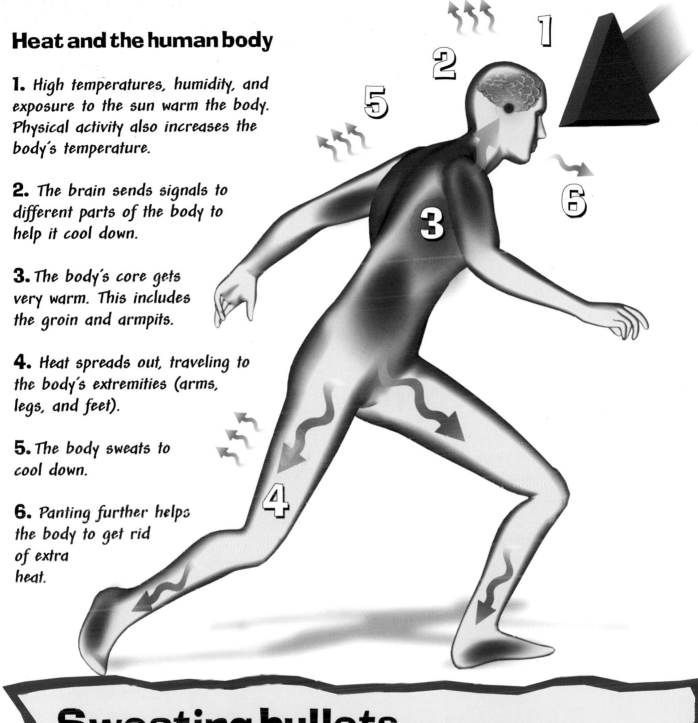

Sweating bullets

The human body is equipped to function in a variety of temperatures. Sweating is one of the ways that the body regulates itself. The evaporation of sweat on the skin produces a cooling effect, lowering the body's temperature in hot weather. Sometimes, this self-regulating system fails, either because the body does not have enough water to produce sweat, or because the air is so moist that sweat cannot evaporate from the skin. Drinking fluids and staying out of the sun help the body to cool itself down.

In a Dry Land

Without the proper management of water resources, droughts and heat waves will continue to devastate the planet. Water conservation and better farming techniques help people to survive in dry lands and deal with water shortages more effectively.

Prevention

Plants and trees play an important role in anchoring the soil so that it does not wash or blow away in the rain or wind. Blowing topsoil means there is less soil to hold moisture in the ground, and support crops. In some parts of the world, entire tree populations have either died or were cut down for fuel or to build homes and furniture.

In tropical countries, logging, cattle ranching, and over population are creating drought conditions in rainforests. Forest land is cleared for use as farmland, but once the trees are gone, the natural rain cycle ends. Drought and poor soils mean the land becomes useless after a couple of years.

Drought-stricken areas are vulnerable to forest fires, which can burn large areas of forest. Several forest fires swept through the countryside of Switzerland during a drought in 2003.

International aid organizations bring water into drought-stricken communities. There are often so many people in need that once help arrives, people must line up for hours to receive water.

Conservation

In many countries where agriculture is the most important part of the economy, farmers have developed ways of collecting and conserving water. In parts of Africa, for example, farmers water their crops by using a method in which small, crescent-shaped mounds are made from a part-soil and part-manure mixture. These mounds allow rainwater and dew to collect so that less fresh water is needed for irrigation. In California, a system of computerized weather stations tell farmers how much moisture is in the soil. The system helps conserve water in a dry climate by allowing farmers to irrigate only when necessary.

In water-rich North America, people are encouraged to monitor and control their water use. During the hot summer months of July and August, many communities have a system in which watering yards, plants, and washing cars is permitted only at certain times and on certain days. Still, North Americans use far more water every day than people in Europe or Africa. When water is cheap and plentiful, people often waste it. In dry countries, water is precious and rarely wasted.

Cool-off areas

In many North American cities and towns, authorities designate certain areas as "cool-off areas." These areas, such as public swimming pools and air-conditioned community centers, are where large numbers of people can go to escape the heat at the same time. Sharing resources saves more energy than when people cool off at their own homes. The use of electric fans and air conditioners places a high demand on hydroelectricity plants during heat waves. It is easier to meet electricity demands when people coordinate and share resources at cooling areas.

(right) A mother and son enjoy a cooling spray on a hot day.

(below) Cool-off areas are set up by community workers and volunteers during severe heat waves.

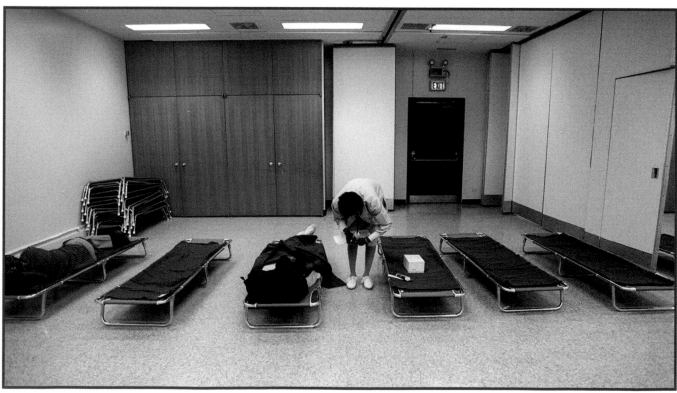

Drought-Resistant Crops

Some plants need little water to grow. Millet and sorghum are cereal crops that have adapted to dry environments. These plants have tough, waxy stalks and leaves which do not allow water to evaporate from them easily. They also have seeds with skins that protect against water loss. On the Great Plains of the United States and the Canadian Prairies, scientists have come up with strains of wheat that grow quickly in dry conditions.

Some mechanical irrigation systems require large amounts of water.

(below) Crop technology is developing all over the world. North American farmers are currently working with new strains of wheat that require little water to grow.

Famine

Famine is when many people starve due to a shortage of food. Some famines are caused by droughts, which ruin harvests, leaving people and livestock without food. Despite assistance from the international community, famines cause the deaths of thousands of people, especially when they last for several years.

Struggling for food

In recent years, many parts of Africa have suffered terrible famines, such as the desert regions of the Sahara and Kalahari. Malnutrition resulting from hunger weakens the population, making it more difficult for people to get the food and water they need to survive. The deaths of livestock means farmers lose their source of income, and leave people without meat and milk. Deaths due to dehydration, disease, and starvation cause the population to shrink, meaning fewer people are left to produce and process food. Famine is caused by drought but is also caused by civil war and war between countries.

Somalians unload a cargo of wheat. In the 1980s and '90s, war between Somalia, the Sudan, and Ethiopia caused widespread famine. People relied on donated food but many still died.

Desertification

Desertification is the gradual spread of desert-like conditions over a large area. As a region becomes more heavily populated, there is a greater need to produce food. Farmers damage the land by trying to grow too many crops too quickly. Overfarming makes the land useless, and the barren soil erodes and spreads. The soil loses the nutrients it needs to stay healthy when too many trees are cut for housing or fuel. Soil that lacks nutrients cannot support food crops. Desertification causes permanent changes to the landscape, forcing people to leave their homes in search of drinking water and arable land.

During times of war, violence disrupts the daily lives of people, making it difficult for them to get food and water from local sources.

International aid

International organizations, such as the Red Cross and Red Crescent, help the victims of famine by bringing food, water, and medicine to the people who need it. Aid workers save thousands of lives in this way. Aside from food and water, relief agencies may provide vitamins to repair bones, skin, and eyesight, and medicines to heal the sick. Relief workers also help to create sanitary conditions, which help to reduce the spread of disease during famine.

People wait in line to receive food rations.

Recipe for Disaster

This activity will allow you to re-create, in miniature form, a real-life water cycle. Once you have built it, you will be able to observe how water interacts with soil, plants, and the atmosphere.

What you need:
* A jar with a lid
* 4 or 5 small live plants or flowers (with roots attached)
* Soil to fill the jar about half full
* 8 to 10 small rocks or pebbles
* Water
* Sand (about half as much as the soil you have collected)
* A bottle cap or shell

What to do:

1. Place the rocks or pebbles in the jar and pour the sand on top. Then add the soil.

2. Plant the flowers or plants in the soil.

3. Fill the bottle cap or shell with water, and place it on an open patch of soil in the jar.

4. Put the lid on the jar, then place your water cycle in a sunny place.

5. Over the next few days, write down your observations about what happens in the jar.

OBSERVATIONS

What you will see:

During the three or four days you are observing the miniature water cycle, the inside of the jar should start to become covered with a mist of evaporated water. The plants should start to grow during this time, without adding any more water to the cap or shell. This is similar to the real-life water cycle, in which water is simply re-cycled for plants to use.

31

Glossary

aboriginal A group of people native to a country or who have lived there from the beginning

advisory A statement issued about bad weather

arable Suitable for growing crops

atmosphere The layers of gases that surround the Earth

catastrophic Describing a sudden disaster and its ruinous effects

cereal crops Crops such as wheat, oats, or corn grown as food

climate The usual weather of an area

compress To squeeze something together

condensation The process in which a gas cools to form a liquid

conservation Protection or management of a valuable resource, such as water

dehydration The process by which the body loses the water it needs to function

erosion The wearing or blowing away of soil

evaporation The process by which a liquid turns to a gas

high pressure Air pressure where winds rotate opposite to the Earth's rotation

infestation Overpopulation of an unwanted pest

irrigation A system in which water is collected from rainfall, streams, and rivers to water crops

low pressure Air pressure where winds rotate in the same direction as the Earth

malnutrition Sickness that comes from not eating enough or eating unhealthy foods

molecules The smallest parts of something

monsoon A seasonal wind that brings heavy rainstorms in the summer months to some parts of the world, especially Asia

overfarming Farming in an area over a long period of time without allowing the soil to regain its nutrients

precipitation Moisture that falls from the sky, including rain and snow

subsurface Under the ground

vital nutrients Important, nourishing or life-giving ingredients in foods

Index

1 2 3 4 5 6 7 8 9 0   Printed in the U.S.A.   3 2 1 0 9 8 7 6 5 4